Chinese Australians

Book 3

Chinese and Gold

The Chinese on the Australian Goldfields

Marji Hill

Published by The Prison Tree Press 2025

Copyright © 2025 Marji Hill

The Prison Tree Press
Suite 124
1-10 Albert Avenue
Broadbeach, Queensland 4218
https://marjihill.com

ISBN: 9781763738461 Hardback
ISBN: 9781763738478 eBook

 A catalogue record for this book is available from the National Library of Australia

All rights reserved. No part of this book may be reproduced, stored in a retrieval system, or transmitted in any form or by any means, electronic, mechanical, photocopying, recording, scanning, or otherwise, without the prior written permission of the publisher.

Disclaimer:

All the material contained in this book is provided for educational and informational purposes only. No responsibility can be taken for any results or outcomes resulting from the use of this material.

While every care has been taken to trace and acknowledge copyright the publishers tender their apologies for any accidental infringement where copyright has proved untraceable.

Every attempt has been made to provide information that is both accurate and effective, however, the author does not assume any responsibility for the accuracy or use/misuse of this information.

Acknowledgement is given to Canva for most of the illustrations in this book. The paintings, however, were created by Marji Hill.

THE SERIES

Chinese Australians

Book 1

Australia and China

Before Captain Cook

Book 2

Early Chinese Migrants

The First Chinese Australians

Book 3

Chinese and Gold

The Chinese on the Australian Goldfields

Book 4

The Chinese Experience

The Untold Story of Prejudice and Violence on the Australian Goldfields

Book 5

The Chinese Legacy

How Migration, Culture and Community have Influenced Australia

Acknowledgements

I acknowledge the Traditional Custodians
of Country throughout Australia
and their connections to land, sea, and community.

I pay my respect to elders, past, present, and emerging
and extend my respect to all First Nations peoples today.
In the spirit of reconciliation,
my mission is to increase understanding
between the First Nations and other Australians
and to provide people from all over the globe
some basic understanding of Australia s first people,
their history, and cultures.

In addition,
I thank Eddie Dowd for helping me get this book
into its final form for publication.
I also acknowledge the support
from John and Sherien Foley.

Marji Hill

Table of Contents

1.	Gold Fever Hits Australia!	1
2.	Australia's Population Booms	3
3.	The Chinese Arrive	5
4.	Life on the goldfields	9
5.	More Than Just Mining	11
6.	Trouble on the Goldfields	13
7.	The Government Steps In	17
8.	Walking From Robe	19
9.	Fighting Back	21
10.	Why Did Some Europeans Dislike the Chinese?	23
11.	Attacks and Riots	25
12.	New Laws Keep Chinese Out	27
13.	Looking Back	29
GLOSSARY		33
SOURCES		35
ABOUT MARJI HILL		37
MORE BOOKS BY MARJI HILL		39

1. Gold Fever Hits Australia!

Imagine digging in the ground and suddenly finding gold—a gold nugget! That is what happened in Australia in 1851.

When word got out that gold had been discovered, people all over the world got excited. The news spread like wildfire, and soon thousands of people sailed across the ocean and came rushing to Australia, dreaming of striking it rich.

People sailed across the ocean to Australia

This rush to find gold was called the gold rush and it completely changed Australia.

By the end of 1851, there were already thousands of people digging for gold near a place called Ballarat in Victoria. Gold had already been found in New South Wales but the finds there were dwarfed by the finds in Victoria.

People came from all over the world—England, Ireland, Europe, China, America, and more. Ships packed with hopeful gold diggers arrived in Melbourne and the search for treasure began!

2. Australia's Population Booms

Before gold was discovered, Australia's population was just over 437,000 in 1851. But within ten years, the population had more than doubled! Over 600,000 people came to Australia between 1851 and 1860. By 1861, the population was more than one million people and more than half of them were in Victoria. This huge population growth was mostly because of the gold rush.

One group that came in large numbers were the Chinese. Almost 40,000 Chinese people arrived in Australia during the gold rush years, hoping to find gold and a better life.

3. The Chinese Arrive

In 1852 alone, more than 3,000 Chinese people came to Australia. By the end of that year, the number had doubled! They called Australia the "New Gold Mountain," hoping it would bring good fortune.

Gold attracted miners from across the world

Most of the Chinese miners came from a densely populated area in southern China called the Pearl River Delta. Life in China was tough at the time, and many people were poor. They were willing to take big risks and travel far from home for the chance to find gold. They were desperate to do whatever it took to improve their lives.

Life in China was tough at the time and many people were poor

But coming to Australia was not cheap. Some Chinese men paid for the journey with their own money. Others borrowed money to pay for their journey. These loans worked like a credit ticket — this meant they borrowed money for the trip and they had to repay it by working in Australia.

Some men even promised their land or asked their families to take responsibility if they could not repay the debt.

Chinese men had to leave their wives and families in China. They hoped to send money home and maybe even return one day with enough savings for a better life.

They travelled to the goldfields dreaming of a better life together with the hope of being able to support their families back in China.

But the journey was long and life in Australia was not easy.

4. Life on the goldfields

Once they arrived, the Chinese miners often functioned in large, organised groups. On the goldfields they worked together in teams supervised by a headman. Usually, they came from the same village in China.

**The days were long
and the work was hard**

They had a reputation for being patient and thorough. While European miners usually rushed from one claim to another, the Chinese returned to dig in areas others had abandoned. With careful teamwork and skill, they were able to find the gold that had been missed from the previously worked claims.

Living and working on the goldfields was tough. There was no such thing as an easy way to avoid the challenges.

The days were long, the work was hard and the living conditions were poor. People lived in tents or simple huts and there was very little comfort.

The Chinese experienced racial hostility, discrimination and prejudice from the Europeans. When they were successful at acquiring gold, jealousies arose.

5. More Than Just Mining

The Chinese were entrepreneurial and they sought out opportunities to make money. They provided services to support those living on the diggings: washing clothes, setting up market gardens, selling cooked food, and supplying herbal medicines.

The Chinese set up market gardens

The Chinese lived in simple, well-organised camps with neat rows of tents or bark huts. They planted vegetable gardens, growing cabbages, beans, onions and other crops. This gave them a healthier diet than many European miners, who mainly ate meat and damper (a type of bread). The Chinese cooked rice, brewed tea, and sometimes sold fresh food to others on the diggings.

As the number of miners from China continued to grow, many Europeans were unhappy and resentful. They questioned why so many of these people were allowed to be in the colony.

This caused arguments, fights, and even violence.

6. Trouble on the Goldfields

The goldfields were noisy, messy, and sometimes dangerous. There were fights, robberies and even riots. The different cultures — English, Irish, Scottish, Chinese and more — did not always get along.

The Chinese were often treated unfairly. European miners did not understand their customs, and some people did not like that the Chinese miners looked and acted differently. This led to even more discrimination and prejudice.

Some Europeans believed the Chinese were taking "their" gold, even though the Chinese mostly searched old mine sites that had already been abandoned.

From 1851 to 1860, the Victorian goldfields were the focus of attention in Australia. Until the discovery of gold in north Queensland later in the century, Victoria was Australia s most important gold producer. From the European perspective, it seemed as though the Chinese were arriving on the Australian goldfields at an alarming rate.

By mid-1855 around 17,000 Chinese were on the goldfields. By 1861, nearly 40,000 Chinese had arrived.

Given the flood of Chinese to the goldfields it was not long before resentment and ill-feeling grew.

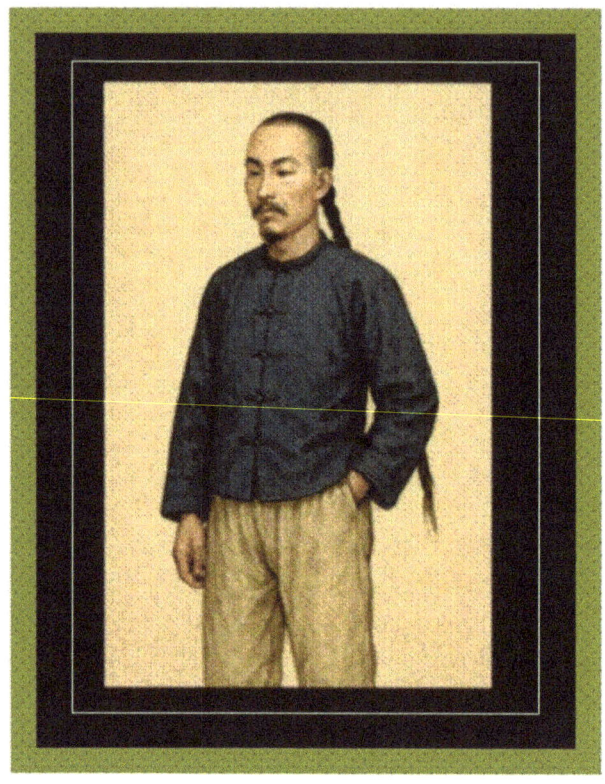

Resentment and ill-feeling grew

The Chinese question became a subject of hot debate both on the goldfields and beyond. The response by the colonial government was to implement poll taxes and restrictions to limit the number of Chinese entering Australia. Both New South Wales (NSW) and Victoria commenced immigration restrictions.

The mass migration of the Chinese to Australia was seen as a security risk. The colonial government feared what might be the possible intentions of the Chinese emperor. In addition, they feared competition on the goldfields.

Even though the Chinese miners reworked old claims that had been deserted by the Europeans these actions still upset the Europeans. The

Chinese were accused of taking their claims and disgruntled diggers blamed the Chinese for all their misfortunes.

7. The Government Steps In

As more Chinese miners arrived, the colonial government decided to make laws to limit their numbers. In 1855, Victoria passed a law called the Chinese Restriction Act. It was the first of its kind in Australia and the British Empire.

This law made Chinese immigrants pay a £10 tax to enter the colony. Ships could only carry one Chinese passenger for every 10 tonnes of cargo. The government even set up "Protectors" to watch over Chinese people and make sure they followed the rules.

Chinese miners were forced to live in separate areas away from the European miners. Similar laws were passed in New South Wales after a major race riot at a place called Lambing Flat in 1860–1861.

These laws were early signs of something bigger, namely, the White Australia Policy. This was a set of rules designed to keep non-Europeans from moving to Australia. This policy lasted until the 1970s!

8. Walking From Robe

To avoid paying the entry tax in Victoria, many Chinese landed in South Australia, in a small town called Robe. They disembarked there, a long way from the Victorian goldfields.

From Robe the Chinese walked hundreds of kilometres to the Victorian goldfields

From Robe, they walked hundreds of kilometres to the Victorian goldfields—a journey that could take three weeks or more!

It was a dangerous trip. There were bushrangers (robbers), harsh weather and wild terrain. Sometimes Chinese travellers left messages on trees in their own language to warn others about dangers ahead.

They would walk in single file, carrying their supplies in baskets balanced on bamboo poles across their shoulders. Groups could be as large as 700 people!

The Chinese miners walked long distances

Travelling in big groups helped them stay safe.

9. Fighting Back

The Chinese did not just sit back and accept unfair treatment. They stood up for themselves with protests and petitions.

In 1857, the Victorian government introduced a new tax: every Chinese person in Victoria had to buy a license for £1 every two months. This made life even harder.

The Chinese miners protested in a big way.

In 1859, thousands marched in Castlemaine, demanding fair treatment. They created groups like the United Confederacy of Chinese and sent a giant petition with thousands of signatures to the government.

10. Why Did Some Europeans Dislike the Chinese?

There were a few reasons why anti-Chinese feelings grew.

Chinese men wore their hair in long pigtails

1. **They looked different:**

    Chinese men wore their hair in long pigtails, had straw hats, and wore long robes or blue padded jackets. They often walked barefoot or wore rope-soled shoes.

2. **Different customs.**

   The Chinese had different religions and lived together in their own communities. They did not bring their women to Australia and this made some people suspicious.

3. **They were good at mining.**

   The Chinese often found gold in places others had given up on. They worked as a team and were very skilled at saving water and reusing tools. This made some European miners jealous.

11. Attacks and Riots

Many Chinese miners were attacked. In 1854, over 1,500 European miners in Bendigo held a meeting to plan how to drive the Chinese out.

One of the worst cases of anti-Chinese violence was the Buckland Valley Riot in 1857. A group of drunken men, many of them Americans, left a local hotel with axe handles and clubs. They joined with others who were ready to drive the Chinese out of the Buckland Valley.

They destroyed tents, robbed Chinese miners and torched their belongings. The newly built Chinese temple was set on fire and burned to the ground.

While there were reports of just a few Chinese men killed, there were also rumours of a much larger massacre. It is believed that many others may have died or been injured as they fled. Chinese tents were set on fire and many of the miners were injured.

More anti-Chinese violence took place at Lambing Flat (now known as the town of Young) in New South Wales (NSW) in June 1861. This anti-Chinese riot was one of the most horrific explosions of racial violence in Australian history, another defining moment in Australia's past. The implications of these events reverberated throughout Australian political and cultural history.

The Buckland Valley and the Lambing Flat riots were not isolated expressions of aggression against the Chinese; there was more Anti-Chinese violence in other areas.

12. New Laws Keep Chinese Out

In 1861, more laws were passed to stop Chinese people from coming to Australia.

In 1888, New South Wales made a new rule: anyone who wanted to move there had to write out a passage in a European language but the immigration officer got to pick which one. It could be French, German or even something the person had never learned!

In 1901, the new federal government passed the Immigration Restriction Act, beginning the White Australia Policy. This policy kept most non-Europeans, including Chinese, from moving to Australia for many years.

It remained the policy for many decades until it was dismantled by the Whitlam government and replaced with the policy of multiculturalism in 1973.

13. Looking Back

The story of the Chinese on the Australian goldfields is full of hope, courage, hard work — and injustice.

These miners faced many challenges, but they also helped shape Australia's history. They showed great resilience. The Chinese helped each other, built strong communities, and found ways to earn a living even when times were tough.

**The Chinese contributed greatly
to the development of Australia**

Even in the face of many obstacles, they contributed greatly to the development of Australia and left behind a lasting legacy that can still be seen today.

Many stayed on in Australia after the gold rush ended, becoming market gardeners, storekeepers, or running small businesses. They introduced new foods, traditions, and cultural practices that enriched Australian society.

The Chinese introduced new foods, traditions, and cultural practices that enriched Australian society

Today, we can remember their efforts and learn from the past. The gold rush brought many people together from different parts of the world — and it is a big part of how modern Australia began.

Life in China was tough in the 1800s - many people were willing to take big risks and travel far from home for the chance to find gold.

GLOSSARY

Credit Ticket — A way of paying for travel using a loan that had to be paid back later.

Diggings — The area where gold miners worked.

Discrimination — Treating people unfairly because they are different in some way.

Entrepreneur — A person who starts a business to make money.

Immigrant — A person who moves to another country to live.

Miner — A person who digs into the ground searching for gold or other precious minerals.

Petition — A written request signed by many people to ask for change.

Poll Tax — A fee people had to pay to enter a country, often used unfairly.

Restriction Act — A law made to control who could come into the country.

White Australia Policy — A group of laws that stopped people from Asia and other non-European countries from moving to Australia.

SOURCES

The author would like to acknowledge the following sources of information:

Hill, Marji 2022 *Gold and the Chinese: Racism, Riots and Protest on the Australian Goldfields.* Broadbeach, Qld, The Prison Tree Press. (Gold! Hidden Stories of Australia's Past, Book 3)

Mo Yimei (1988) "Harvest of Endurance: a History of the Chinese in Australia 1788-1988" Sydney, Australia-China Friendship Society. http://www.multiculturalaustralia.edu.au/doc/yimei_1.pdf

ABOUT MARJI HILL

Marji Hill runs her art career alongside her career as an author. She is a highly respected international author as well as a seasoned business executive, researcher and coach.

Marji is passionate about promoting understanding between Australia's First Nations people and other Australians. The spirit of reconciliation was fostered in all her writings ever since she was a Research Fellow in Education at the Australian Institute of Aboriginal and Torres Strait Islander Studies (AIATSIS) in Canberra.

From 2008 to 2011, Marji was Deputy Chairperson of the Mosman Branch of Reconciliation Australia in Sydney. Following her Research Fellowship at AIATSIS in 1976 Marji, together with her late partner, Alex Barlow, produced more than seventy (70) books on all aspects of the First Nations people including the critical, annotated bibliography *Black Australia*.

In 1989 she was the Project Coordinator and one of the researchers and writers of *Australian Aboriginal Culture* the official Australian Government publication on First Nations people.

In 1988 *Six Australian Battlefields* was published by Angus and Robertson. A decade later it was re-published by Allen & Unwin as a paperback edition. Her nine-volume encyclopaedia, *Macmillan Encyclopaedia of Australia's Aboriginal Peoples* was published in 2000 and in 2009 she published *The Apology: Saying Sorry To The Stolen Generations*.

Marji's more recent publications extend to self-improvement and self-help with books like *Staying Young Growing Old* and *Inspired by Country* a self-help book about painting with gouache.

MORE BOOKS BY MARJI HILL

First Nations

Hill, Marji 2021 *Australian Aboriginal History: 5 Stories of Indigenous Heroes.* Broadbeach, Qld, The Prison Tree Press.

Hill, Marji 2021 *First People Then and Now: Introducing Indigenous Australians.* 2nd ed. Broadbeach, Qld, The Prison Tree Press.

Aboriginal Global Pioneers

Hill, Marji 2024 *Australian Aboriginal Origins: Earliest Beginnings.* Broadbeach, Qld, The Prison Tree Press. (Book 1)

Hill, Marji 2024 *Australian Aboriginal Trade: Sharing Goods and Services.* Broadbeach, Qld, The Prison Tree Press. (Book 2)

Hill, Marji 2024 *Australian Aboriginal Religion: Country and Dreaming.* Broadbeach, Qld, The Prison Tree Press. (Book 3)

Hill, Marji 2024 *Australian Aboriginal Fire: Managing Country.* Broadbeach, Qld, The Prison Tree Press. (Book 4)

Hill, Marji 2024 *Australian Aboriginal Medicine: Caring for People.* Broadbeach, Qld, The Prison Tree Press. (Book 5)

Self-improvement/Self-Help

Hill, Marji 2014 *Staying Young Growing Old.* Broadbeach, Qld, The Prison Tree Press.

Hill, Marji 2020 *How Big Is Your Why? An Author's Guide to Time Management and Productivity to Achieve Transformational Results.* Broadbeach, Qld, The Prison Tree Press.

Hill, Marji 2020 *A Create and Publish Toolbox: 101 Prompts In A Guided Journal To Help You Write, Self-publish, And Market Your Book on Amazon.* Broadbeach, Qld, The Prison Tree Press.

Hill, Marji 2021 *Inspired by Country: An Artist's Journey Back to Nature, Landscape Painting with Gouache.* Broadbeach, Qld, The Prison Tree Press.

Hill, Marji 2024 *Australian Paintings: Artworks by Marji Hill.* Broadbeach, Qld, The Prison Tree Press.

Gold

Hill, Marji 2022 *Gates of Gold: The Discovery of Gold, its Legacy and its Contribution to Australian Identity.* Broadbeach, Qld, The Prison Tree Press.

Hill, Marji 2022 *Shadows of Gold: Eureka and the Birth of Australian Democracy.* Broadbeach, Qld, The Prison Tree Press.

Hill, Marji 2022 *Gold and the Chinese: Racism, Riots and Protest on the Australian Goldfields.* Broadbeach, Qld, The Prison Tree Press.

Hill, Marji 2022 *Ghosts of Gold: The Life and Times of Jupiter Mosman.* Broadbeach, Qld, The Prison Tree Press.

Hill, Marji 2022 *Blood Gold: Native Police, Bushrangers & Law and Order on the Goldfields.* Broadbeach, Qld, The Prison Tree Press.

www.ingramcontent.com/pod-product-compliance
Lightning Source LLC
Chambersburg PA
CBHW041218240426
43661CB00012B/1084